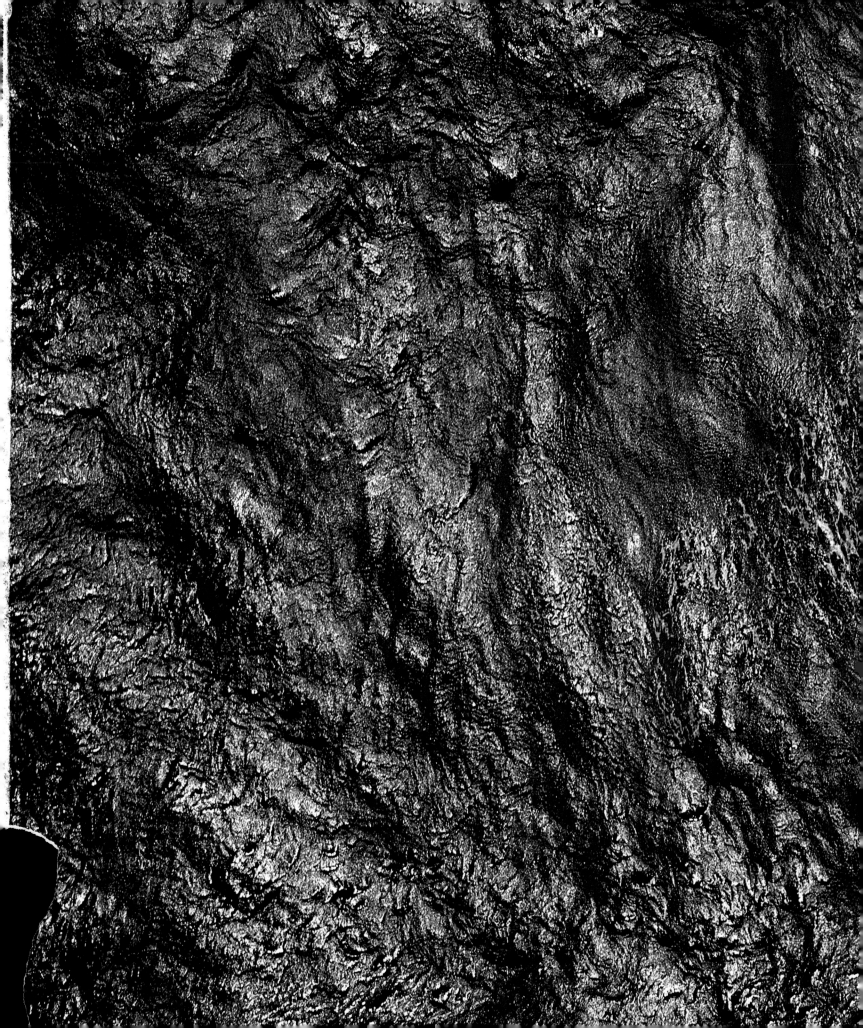

CREATIVE EDUCATION

OCEAN RESOURCES

JENNY MARKERT

Designed by Rita Marshall
with the help of Thomas Lawton

Published by Creative Education
123 South Broad Street,
Mankato, Minnesota 56001
Creative Education is an imprint
of Creative Education, Inc.

Photography by Peter Arnold, Inc.
(B. Evans, Michael Fairchild), Carr
Clifton, Comstock (George Lepp,
Franklin Viola), F-Stock (Larry
Pierce), Photo Researchers (Wesley
Bocxe, Douglas Faulkner, Spencer
Grant, Michael Kuh, Rondi/Tani)
and Tom Stack & Associates (Scott
Blackman, Gerald & Buff Corsi,
M. Timothy O'Keefe, Brian Parker,
Denise Tackett)

Library of Congress
Cataloging-in-Publication Data

Markert, Jenny.
Ocean resources / Jenny Markert.
Summary: Discusses the world's
oceans as a source of food, fresh
water, minerals, and energy.
ISBN 0-88682-599-7
1. Marine resources—Juvenile
literature. [1. Marine resources.]
I. Title.   93-12204
GC1016.5.M37 1993   CIP
333.91'64—dc20   AC

7

The future poses many challenges for humankind. A rapidly growing world population is making increasing demands on limited food and water resources. Between 1950 and 1991, the world's population more than doubled, from 2.5 billion to 5.4 billion. Statisticians estimate there will be 8.2 billion people vying for the necessities of life by the year 2025. With every day that passes, we are using up our planet's remaining mineral and energy resources, while at the same time polluting the soil, water, and air.

Anchovy feeding in Monterey Bay, California.

Covering 70 percent of our planet, however, is a vast resource that we have only begun to tap: the world's ocean. If we respect its treasures and carefully uncover its secrets, the *Ocean* can provide us with such essentials as food, water, minerals, and energy.

One of the ocean's most obvious and important resources is *Food*. For thousands of years, people living on ocean shores have depended on the sea for fish, shellfish, and marine plants. Today, the ocean supplies food for much of the inland world as well. Organized fishing fleets sweep the seas with nets, yielding 75 million tons (68 million t) of seafood every year. Their catches include halibut, shrimp, tuna, cod, and herring. Clams, lobsters, and oysters are also harvested from the sea.

A commercial fishing boat off the Oregon coast.

Not very long ago, people believed the ocean contained more fish than we could ever catch. But in reality, the ocean's food reserves are not unlimited. Just in the last century, fishing fleets have greatly reduced the numbers of fish in the world's ocean. If we continue fishing at the rate we do today, we may wipe out all traces of tuna, herring, cod, and many other forms of sea life. Many species of whales already have been hunted to the point of extinction. Other sea creatures, such as dolphins, are destroyed by accident. Dolphins are mammals that breathe oxygen from the air. Each year, more than 150,000 dolphins drown when they become tangled in the nets used to catch tuna.

A school of fusiliers in Celebes Sea, East Malaysia.

13

One method for feeding our growing population while ensuring the survival of sea life is *Aquaculture,* or underwater farming. Just as we raise animals and plants on land, we have begun to raise sea life in the ocean. Aquaculture began in Asia centuries ago. Today it is used worldwide to provide about 10 percent of the world's fish and shellfish.

Plant aquaculture, in particular, may become an increasingly important food source for future generations. Seaweed products have been used for years to bind together blended foods such as salad dressings and ice cream. Ocean plants offer many other benefits as well. They are quite versatile and can be flavored to taste like meat or vegetables. They grow rapidly and are rich in the nutrients potassium and iodine. Furthermore, many ocean plants are more than 50 percent protein. These plants are a much more efficient source of protein than animals and poultry, which must eat large quantities of plants to produce the protein we eat in meat.

Giant kelp.

In addition to its growing need for food, humankind also has a growing need for *Fresh Water*. It is hard to believe that water is in short supply on a planet where more than two-thirds of the surface is covered by water. But because ocean water is salty, it is useless for drinking and agriculture. To be used by humans, the salty water that fills the ocean must be converted into fresh water in a process called *Desalination*. In the simplest method of desalination, glass-covered tanks are filled with seawater and placed in the sunlight. Heated by the sun, the seawater evaporates and leaves the salts behind. Water vapor rises into the air and condenses on the glass covering, similar to the way water in your breath condenses when you breathe on a cold window. This salt-free water runs off the glass and is collected in reservoirs.

Sea salt, produced by the evaporation of seawater.

Desalination plants currently provide fresh water to the Virgin Islands, Bermuda, and other small islands that receive little rain, as well as to desert countries such as Kuwait. As the earth's population continues to grow, future generations will increasingly rely on desalinated ocean water for supplying homes with water, irrigating crops, and manufacturing products. New, more efficient technologies must be developed, however, since producing a steady supply of desalinated water uses a great amount of energy.

Solar salt pans.

The ocean provides humankind with other resources besides food and fresh water. After purifying salty seawater, we are left with *Sodium Chloride*, or common table salt, used to flavor countless foods. Although sodium chloride is the most abundant mineral dissolved in seawater, other useful substances can also be found in significant quantities. For instance, more than half of the world's supply of magnesium, an important metal used in photography and construction, is extracted from ocean water. Bromine, used to make motor fuels, and smaller amounts of gypsum, potassium, and iodine can be extracted from ocean water as well.

Salt extraction in Spain.

In fact, seawater contains every element found on land, including valuable ones such as gold and silver. Most of these elements are not extracted from seawater, however, because they can be mined more cheaply on land. For example, all seawater contains gold, but the cost of filtering the precious metal from the water would far exceed the value of the gold obtained.

While many valuable minerals are dissolved in the ocean's waters, other important materials lie on the ocean floor. The most accessible of these materials are sand and gravel, which cover much of the continental shelves (underwater plains that form the edges of the continents). In a process called *Dredging*, gigantic scoops scrape the ocean bottom and carry these materials to the surface. The sand and gravel dredged from the sea are used in coastal areas for constructing buildings and roads.

Gravel on the sea bottom.

Some areas of the deep ocean floor contain *Manganese Nodules,* which look like flat coins or dense lumps of coal. In some places, they cover the entire seafloor like cobblestones on a road. The largest deposit of manganese nodules ever found is 16,000 feet (4,877 m) below the surface of the North Pacific. It is thousands of miles long and contains billions of tons of nodules.

❧

Manganese nodules are valuable because they are rich in manganese and iron and contain smaller amounts of useful elements such as copper, nickel, and cobalt. Unfortunately, mining the nodules is an expensive task that requires complicated equipment and specially designed ships. One way the nodules are retrieved is with gigantic vacuumlike devices, which suck the nodules through long tubes to the ocean surface. Another method, similar to taking water from a well, involves sending a continuous chain of buckets down to the ocean depths. The buckets scrape the nodules off the seafloor and carry them up to the ocean surface.

Page 22: Sand ripples in shallow water.
Page 23: The exotic ocean floor.

Currently, the minerals found in manganese nodules are mined separately on land. As these land supplies gradually become depleted and as methods for mining the deep ocean floor become more efficient, manganese nodules may become an important source of valuable minerals.

The stark Pacific coast at La Push, Washington.

The most sought-after ocean resources are *Oil* and *Natural Gas*—sources of energy that power our cars, heat our homes, and light our cities. The ocean's reserves of oil and natural gas do not float in its waters or lie on its floor; instead, they are buried far beneath the ocean bottom. Tapping these pools of oil and gas is not an easy task. Before drilling is even considered, specialists discuss financial, technical, and environmental concerns. After they have located a promising site, drilling rigs poke into the ocean floor. Sometimes the rigs come up empty, uncovering water or only small amounts of oil or gas. When a significant reserve eventually is located, a production platform is built, and the oil or gas reserves are tapped.

About 20 percent of the world's oil and 5 percent of its natural gas come from beneath the ocean floor. Some scientists think that the reserves that lie beneath the ocean floor may exceed all the oil and natural gas we have found on land. With current land supplies quickly diminishing, ocean reserves will become more and more important.

Offshore oil rigs and the setting sun, Santa Barbara, California.

Unfortunately, extracting oil and natural gas from the ocean floor can have a very negative effect on the environment. Even at current production levels, as much as two million tons of oil leak into the sea each year. The oil kills many of the surrounding area's plants and animals. In some parts of the world, the damage is long-lasting. Oil spilled in the ocean generally degrades, or decomposes, over several months, but cold temperatures slow nature's chemical and biological processes. The time doubles with each ten-degree drop in temperature. An oil spill in the Arctic Ocean, for example, could have an effect on the environment for up to ten years.

A casualty of an oil spill.

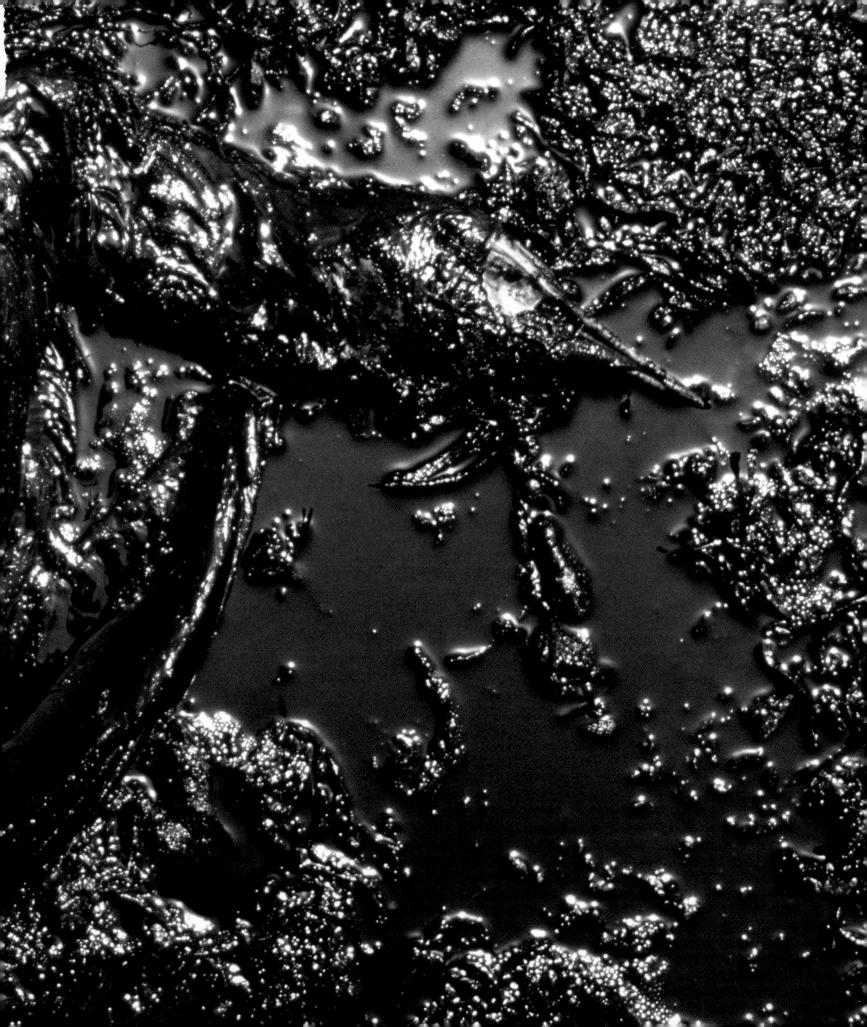

30

At this crucial period in our planet's history, the ocean offers us other sources of energy that do not threaten the environment. One of these is the constant movement of tides, waves, and currents. Scientists have begun to devise methods for harnessing these immense movements of water to generate electricity, called *Hydroelectric Power*.

Trying to contain an oil spill in the aftermath of the Gulf War.

The *Tides* are the most easily harnessed source of energy in the sea. In certain bays and inlets, changes in the tide can generate significant amounts of energy. Modern tidal power stations trap ocean water in the marine basin at high tide and allow it to flow back into the sea during low tide. The flow of the water filling and emptying the basin is used to drive hydraulic turbines that run electric generators. Many countries, including Canada, Great Britain, Mexico, Argentina, India, Korea, and Australia, have areas suited to the development of hydroelectric power from the ocean. In many locations, however, tidal power stations are not economical to operate. For this reason, development was halted on the U.S. tidal station in Passamaquoddy Bay off the Maine coast.

The living ocean.

Although ocean tides generate significant amounts of energy, ocean *Waves* and *Currents* are far more powerful. It is more difficult, however, to convert these movements of water into electricity. The first project to successfully harness the power of waves was completed in Norway in the mid-1980s. Methods for capturing the energy of ocean currents have been proposed but have yet to be attempted.

Waves off the shore of Maui, the Hawaiian Islands.

As the technologies for harnessing the ocean's energy improve, hydroelectric power from the sea may become an important source of energy. Unlike oil, hydroelectric power does not contaminate the environment with choking pollution or dangerous by-products. Another advantage of hydroelectric power is its unlimited availability. Tides receive most of their energy from the gravitational pull of the moon, and waves and currents are powered by the push of the wind. While the world's oil and natural gas supplies will eventually run dry, hydroelectric power will be available as long as we inhabit the earth.

The limitless energy of the ocean.

Since ancient times, areas rich in natural resources—whether on land or sea—have been claimed and defended by the most powerful nations. But the ocean's resources must not be monopolized by one nation or one people; they should benefit all peoples and all forms of life. In 1982, in recognition of this ideal, 119 nations signed an international agreement stating that the ocean and its resources cannot be claimed by any nation. Coastal nations were granted limited rights to ocean resources within 200 miles (322 km) of their coasts, as well as to those resources found on or under the continental shelf that extends beyond 200 miles. The rest of the ocean is protected by a 1970 international resolution stating that the ocean floor is the "common heritage of mankind."

The cooperation of all nations is essential in developing and protecting the ocean's resources.